Anne Frank

Alexandra Zapruder

NATIONAL GEOGRAPHIC

Washington, D.C.

For Hannah and Toby, with all my love

Special thanks to Gracie Corbett for her great enthusiasm and help.
The publisher and author gratefully acknowledge the expert review of this book by
Thomas B. Allen, co-author of the encyclopedia *World War II*.

Alexandra Zapruder was on the founding staff of the United States Holocaust Memorial Museum and is the author of *Salvaged Pages: Young Writers' Diaries of the Holocaust*. She is working on a narrative history of the Zapruder film, her grandfather's home movie of the Kennedy assassination.

Paperback ISBN: 978-1-4263-1352-3
Library ISBN: 978-1-4263-1353-0

Book design by YAY! Design

Photo credits
Cover (portrait and detail of plaid journal): Photo by Anne Frank Fonds/Anne Frank House via Getty Images; header throughout (journal entry): EPA/Ade Johnson/Newscom; 1, 15 (inset): Jewish Museum Frankfurt/Anne Frank Fonds Basel/dpa/Corbis; 2, 5, 8, 19, 22, 24 (background), 24 (top left), 24 (bottom left and right), 25, 27, 31 (including inset), 34, 38: Photo by Anne Frank Fonds/Anne Frank House via Getty Images; 5, 32, 42, 45 (image of pen): Shutterstock; 6, 11, 18, 36, 47 (center left and bottom right): Bettmann/Corbis; 7 (inset): Bernard Judd, courtesy of the United States Holocaust Memorial Museum Photo Archives; 7: Todd Gipstein/Corbis; 9, 47 (top right): Hulton-Deutsch Collection/Corbis; 10: Joshua Roberts/Getty Images; 12 (top): Linda Steward/E+/Getty Images; 12 (bottom): Lambert/Archive Photos/Getty Images; 13 (top): PhotoQuest/Getty Images; 13 (center): Catalin Petolea/Shutterstock; 13 (bottom): Lawrence Manning/Corbis; 14–15: Kimberley Coole/Getty Images; 20: Michael Jenner/Robert Harding World Imagery/Getty Images; 26: Eva Schloss, courtesy of the United States Holocaust Memorial Museum Photo Archives; 28: Leo La Valle/epa/Corbis; 32: Brittany Courville/Shutterstock; 33: Photo by Galerie Bilderwelt/Getty Images; 35, 46 (top): Roger Viollet/Getty Images; 41: Luca Teuchmann/WireImage/Getty Images; 42: Felicitas Garda Collection, courtesy of the United States Holocaust Memorial Museum Photo Archives; 43 (top): Peter Feigl Collection, courtesy of the United States Holocaust Memorial Museum Photo Archives; 43 (center right): Miriam Korber Bercovici Collection, courtesy of the United States Holocaust Memorial Museum Photo Archives; 43 (bottom): Yad Vashem—The Holocaust Martyrs' and Heroes Remembrance Authority; 43 (center left): Cilia Jurer Rudashevsky, courtesy of the United States Holocaust Memorial Museum Photo Archives; 44: Ulrich Baumgarten/Getty Images; 46 (top left): Keystone/Getty Images; 46 (center right): Tomasz Pietryszek/E+/Getty Images; 46 (bottom left): Dick Luria/Taxi/Getty Images; 46 (bottom right): Horace Abrahams/Keystone/Getty Images; 47 (top left): Popperfoto/Getty Images; 47 (bottom left): David Crausby/Alamy

Printed in the United States of America
13/WOR/1

Table of Contents

Who Was Anne Frank? 4

Childhood in Germany 8

In Her Time 12

Life in Holland 14

World War II 16

Into Hiding 20

Inside the Secret Annex 22

Anne's Diary 28

Capture 32

End of the War 36

Finding Anne's Diary 38

6 Other Young Writers 42

A Changed World 44

Glossary 46

Index 48

Who Was
Anne Frank?

Can you imagine being punished just for being who you are? Or because you look, think, or feel differently from those around you?

This is what happened to many people in Europe in the 1930s and '40s. It started when a group called Nazis (NOT-sees) took over the country of Germany under the leadership of a man named Adolf Hitler. The Nazis changed laws to control people's lives. They hated many people, but they treated Jews worst of all. The Nazis told Jews where they could go and what they could do. Many Jews no longer felt safe even in their own homes.

Words to Know

NAZIS: A group of people who followed the ideas of a German leader named Adolf Hitler

JEWS: Those born into a Jewish family or who practice the religion of Judaism

A huge crowd of Nazi soldiers gathers to hear Adolf Hitler speak in Germany in 1936.

Anne Frank was born into a German Jewish family. Her family moved from Germany to Holland to escape the Nazis. But when she was 11 years old, the Nazis attacked Holland. She and her family hid from them for almost two years. During that time, she kept a diary. She wrote almost every day about her life, thoughts, and feelings.

Years later, Anne Frank's diary was published and read by millions. Even though she was a teenager, her diary helped many people—even grown-ups—understand how she and others felt during this time.

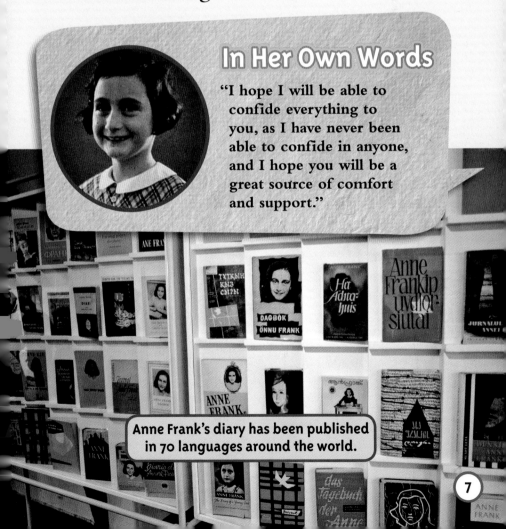

In Her Own Words

"I hope I will be able to confide everything to you, as I have never been able to confide in anyone, and I hope you will be a great source of comfort and support."

Anne Frank's diary has been published in 70 languages around the world.

Childhood in Germany

Anne, Margot, and their mother in Germany in 1933

Anne Frank was born in Germany in 1929. She lived with her parents, Edith and Otto Frank, and her older sister, Margot. Anne's relatives had lived in Germany for a long time. For her family, being Jewish was important, and so was being German.

When Anne was three, Adolf Hitler took power in Germany. He was a dictator who blamed the Jews for Germany's problems. He gave speeches to huge crowds. His followers, the Nazis, made sure his ideas were always on the radio and in the newspapers. Over time, Hitler convinced many people that he was right. Others went along because they were scared of what would happen to them if they disagreed.

Words to Know

DICTATOR: A leader who makes all the rules for a country and controls its people

Adolf Hitler

The Nazis were anti-Semitic (AN-tye-suh-MET-ik). That means they hated Jews. They also punished people who did not want Adolf Hitler to be their leader. They made life terrible for anyone who didn't fit into their idea of what a German citizen should be like. Many people, especially Jews, suddenly became outsiders in their own country.

The Nazis used an ancient figure called a swastika (SWAHS-tik-uh) as their symbol. They put it everywhere—on flags, uniforms, posters, and buildings. For thousands of years before, the swastika was a symbol for good. But the Nazis used it to frighten people and show them that they were in charge of Germany.

Nazi soldiers make arrests.

Anne's parents no longer felt safe in Germany. They wanted to get their family away from the Nazis. They moved to the nearby country of Holland, hoping to find safety there.

In Her Time

Anne Frank was a young girl in the 1930s in Germany. Many things were very different in her world from how they are today.

Staying in Touch

Few people used telephones. Instead, they wrote letters and mailed them. If they needed to reach someone right away, they could send a telegram, a written message delivered quickly.

Fun

For fun, kids read books, played outside, and went to the movies with friends. There were no computers or video games.

World Events

It was a hard time in America and Europe. Millions of people lost their jobs and suddenly became very poor. Many people couldn't even afford to buy bread. This time period is called the Great Depression (di-PRESH-un).

Food

In Germany, strudel (STROOD-ul) was a favorite dessert. It is a pastry filled with fruit. People still eat it today.

News

People got most of their news by listening to the radio or reading newspapers. Most people had never seen a TV.

Life in Holland

Anne's family found a home in the city of Amsterdam (AM-ster-dam). Anne and Margot learned to speak Dutch, the language of Holland, and went to school. Anne had many friends. Some were Jewish and others were not. She went to birthday parties and the movies, and she

Anne Frank and her family lived in a house like this in Amsterdam.

played ping-pong. On her 13th birthday, she began writing her diary.

Anne was curious and loved to talk. Once, when her teacher scolded her for talking, she got out of trouble by writing funny stories about a "chatterbox."

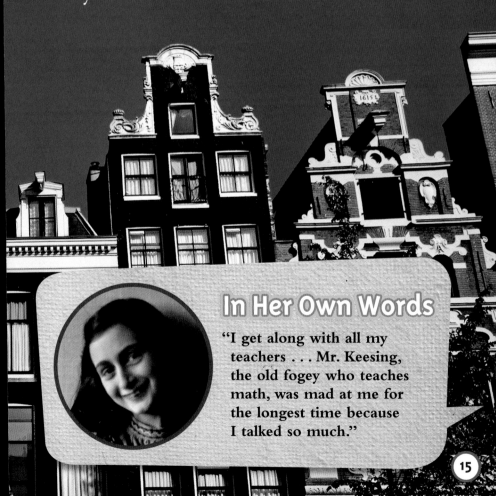

In Her Own Words

"I get along with all my teachers . . . Mr. Keesing, the old fogey who teaches math, was mad at me for the longest time because I talked so much."

World War II

Adolf Hitler and the Nazis wanted to rule all of Europe. They began taking over nearby countries. Then, on September 1, 1939, the German army attacked Poland. Great Britain and France declared war on Germany to defend Poland and try to stop Hitler. World War II had begun.

Meanwhile in the Pacific Ocean, there were other battles brewing. Japan wanted to rule all of East Asia. Countries far away from the Germans were falling under Japanese control. On December 7, 1941, the Japanese bombed the United States naval base Pearl Harbor in Hawaii. The next day, the United States declared war on Japan, and soon after joined Great Britain in fighting Nazi Germany and the other Axis countries.

= German invasion of another country

Norway
Denmark
Netherlands
United Kingdom
Belgium
Luxembourg
France
GERMANY
Poland
Soviet Union (Russia)
Yugoslavia
Greece

The Two Sides

Germany invaded many countries in Europe during the war. They and the countries that fought on their side were called the Axis Powers. The Americans, British, and Russians worked together to defeat them. They were called the Allies. The two sides fought a bitter war for six years and millions died.

Words to Know

INVADE: To enter and try to take over a place, often by force

17

✡ Separating Jews

The Nazis did everything they could to segregate Jews. They forced them to wear a yellow star with the word JEW on their clothing so that everyone would know who was Jewish.

Words to Know

SEGREGATE: To separate someone or something from others

In May 1940, the Germans invaded Holland. Right away, the Nazis passed laws to take away the rights of Jews and other people.

Jews were no longer allowed to own bicycles, go to the movies, or walk in public parks. They could not even visit non-Jewish friends. The Nazis had all of the power. They could do whatever they wanted. Jews lived in constant fear of being arrested, beaten, or killed.

Then the Nazis made plans to send the Jews away from Holland. No one knew where they would be going.

In Her Own Words

"Our freedom was severely restricted by a series of anti-Jewish decrees . . . You couldn't do this and you couldn't do that, but life went on."

Into Hiding

In Her Own Words

"Margot and I started packing our most important belongings into a schoolbag. The first thing I stuck in was this diary, then curlers, handkerchiefs, schoolbooks, a comb and some old letters . . . I stuck the craziest things in the bag . . ."

The building where the Franks hid in Amsterdam is now a museum called the Anne Frank House.

On July 5, 1942, Margot got a "call-up" notice. This meant the Nazis planned to take her away. The family refused to be separated. They went into hiding instead.

Anne's parents had been preparing their hiding place for many months. They called it the Secret Annex (AN-eks). It was attached to a warehouse and the entrance was behind a cupboard. Four workers from Mr. Frank's business helped the family.

Anne had to pack and leave in a hurry. She did not know what it would be like in hiding or if she would ever have a normal life again.

bed

bed

bed

sofa

landing

swinging cupboard

One floor of the Secret Annex, a building attached to the warehouse

Inside the Secret Annex

The Frank family was first to arrive in the hiding place. A week later, they were joined by a couple named Mr. and Mrs. van Pels and their son, Peter.

At first Anne and Margot shared a room. Anne decorated the walls with photos of movie stars.

In Her Own Words

"Up to now our bedroom . . . was very bare. Thanks to Father—who brought my entire postcard and movie star collection here . . . I was able to plaster the walls with pictures. It looks much more cheerful."

Anne's bedroom in the Secret Annex is pictured here in the Anne Frank House.

Bep Voskuijl

Miep Gies

Heroes Who Helped

Miep, Bep, and the other helpers often brought food, clothing, and supplies. It was very dangerous to aid Jews in hiding. If the Nazis found out, those who helped the Franks would be punished.

Johannes Kleiman

Victor Kugler

Daily life was hard. Anne was only rarely allowed to open a window. And she could never ever go outside.

After a few months, a man named Fritz Pfeffer (PFEFF-er) came to hide in the Secret Annex, too. Margot moved into their parents' room and Anne had to share her room

Fritz Pfeffer

with him. Instead of a bed, she slept on two chairs pushed together.

In Her Own Words

"Not being able to go outside upsets me more than I can say, and I'm terrified our hiding place will be discovered . . ."

Eight people lived in a cramped place with the constant fear of being caught. If the Nazis found them, they would be arrested and probably killed. A few times, they almost got caught. These were terrifying moments.

They had to share everything, even one small bathroom. Sometimes they complained and argued with each other.

In Her Own Words

"Footsteps in the house, the private office, the kitchen, then . . . on the staircase. All sounds of breathing stopped, eight hearts pounded . . . Then we heard a can fall, and the footsteps receded. We were out of danger, so far!"

Pictured in the Anne Frank House, this room was shared as a living room and dining room, but was also the bedroom of the van Pels family.

There were many rules to keep the hiding place safe. They had to stay away from windows so no one would see them. They had to be quiet all day. They couldn't even flush the toilet until the warehouse workers left at night. They always had to be careful.

Anne's Diary

Anne's diary was like a best friend during these scary times. She even gave her diary the name "Kitty."

It wasn't easy growing up in hiding. Even though she was surrounded by people, Anne felt alone. Her friends were gone. She couldn't play like other kids. Sometimes she argued with her parents and sister. Other times, she felt like everyone was bossing her around. When Anne got fed up, she told her diary how she felt.

dat die man leuk

Dit is een foto, zoals ik me zou wensen, altijd zo te zijn. Dan had ik nog wel een kans om naar Holywood te komen. Maar tegenwoordig zie ik er jammer genoeg meestal anders uit

Anne dreamed of being a writer
when she grew up. Sometimes she felt
discouraged, but she didn't give up.
She kept working toward her goal of
being a real writer.

Anne described what it was like
to hide from the Nazis. She paid
attention and wrote down the details
in her diary.

One day, Anne heard on the radio
that people were planning to collect
diaries after the war. She thought
people might want to read her diary,
too. So she worked even harder
on her writing than before.

In Her Own Words

"I really believe, Kit, that I'm a little nutty today, and I don't know why. My writing's all mixed up, I'm jumping from one thing to another, and sometimes I seriously doubt whether anyone will ever be interested in this drivel."

Capture

On August 4, 1944, the worst fears of the Frank family came true. At about 10:30 a.m., a group of Nazis burst into the hiding place. They arrested everyone, including two of the helpers. The Nazis sent the hiders to Westerbork, a concentration camp in Holland. One month later, they were sent on a terrible three-day train ride to Auschwitz-Birkenau (OW-shvits BERK-in-ow), a camp in Poland.

Words to Know

CONCENTRATION CAMP: A place where Nazis held Jews and others. Many people were killed or died there.

Auschwitz-Birkenau

One well-known concentration camp was Auschwitz-Birkenau in Poland. Anne Frank, her sister, and mother were among millions of people sent there. When a train arrived, those who were young, old, or looked too sick to work were taken away and killed. The others entered the camp, where guards took their clothes and all their possessions. They shaved the prisoners' heads and gave each one a striped uniform. Prisoners worked all day at hard labor. At night, they were crowded into hard bunks with a single blanket for several people. There was almost no food and people died of terrible hunger and sickness.

Jews from Hungary arrive at Auschwitz-Birkenau in June 1944.

Arriving in the camp was terrifying. It was dark and guards carrying whips yelled orders at people. They separated the men and women. Anne, her mother, and sister ended up together, but they never saw their father, the van Pels, or Fritz Pfeffer again.

Later, Anne and Margot were sent together without their mother to the Bergen–Belsen (BEAR-gin BELL-zin) camp. They both got sick and died of a disease called typhus in March 1945, about two months before the end of the war.

Of the eight people who had been in hiding, only Anne's father, Otto Frank, survived.

Otto Frank

Barbed wire and high fences kept prisoners from escaping from the concentration camps.

End of the War

The Allied American, British, and Russian armies defeated the Germans in World War II. Adolf Hitler died on April 30, 1945, and the war in Europe ended on May 8. The Allied soldiers also entered the concentration camps and liberated the prisoners. The Nazi period of terror was over, but Europe would be torn apart for many years to come.

Survivors of a concentration camp at Ebensee, Austria. U.S. soldiers liberated the camp on May 7, 1945.

It took a long time for people to recover from what had happened to them. Many of them had lost everything—their homes, their jobs, their families and friends. It was difficult to start over with almost nothing. But people slowly rebuilt their lives.

Words to Know

LIBERATE: To set free

DEFEAT: To win a war, battle, or contest against a person, group, or country

Finding Anne's Diary

Anne's writing desk in the Secret Annex

June 12, 1929

Anne Frank born in Frankfurt, Germany

January 1933

Hitler becomes chancellor of Germany

By February 1934

All of the Frank family has moved to Holland

Miep, who had helped the Franks, found Anne's diary in the hiding place. She gathered her notebooks, papers, and the diary and put them in a safe place. She hoped that Anne would come back at the end of the war to get them.

Anne never came back. But her father, Otto, did. He found out after the war that his wife and two daughters had died. He was terribly sad and alone. Then Miep gave him Anne's diary and papers. He read them and decided to make Anne's dream of being a published writer come true.

May 1940
Germans invade Holland

July 6, 1942
Franks go into hiding

August 4, 1944
People in Secret Annex arrested, sent to Auschwitz one month later

Anne's diary was published in 1947.
Since then, millions have read it. Her diary
inspired a play and a movie. There have
been schools and streets named after her.
There is even a museum in the building
where she hid.

Through her diary, Anne Frank told people
what it was like to live in hiding. She
shared things that we would not know if
she hadn't written them down. She was
young, but she helped many people—
including grown-ups—understand an
important part of our history.

October 1944

Anne and Margot
sent to Bergen-Belsen.
Edith Frank forced to
stay at Auschwitz.

January 6, 1945

Edith Frank dies
at Auschwitz

January 27, 1945

Auschwitz liberated
by Russian army.
Otto Frank is freed.

Children visit a reconstruction of Anne in the Secret Annex at a wax museum in Berlin.

March 1945
Anne and Margot die at Bergen-Belsen

June 3, 1945
Otto Frank returns to Amsterdam

Summer 1947
Anne's diary first published in Amsterdam

6 Other Young Writers

Anne Frank wasn't the only teenager to keep a diary. Many others did, too. Some hid like she did. Some left their homes to find safety. Others lived in ghettos. Each diary helps us understand more about life during this terrible time.

Words to Know

GHETTO: A closed-off area, usually in a Polish town or city, where the Nazis forced Jews to live together

Fifteen-year-old Otto Wolf hid in a forest with his sister and parents. He wrote almost every day for three years. He was killed shortly before the end of the war. His sister and parents survived.

2 Peter Feigl started his diary in hiding in France at age 13. He hid for nearly two years, helped by Catholic, Quaker, and Protestant rescuers. He escaped to Switzerland and settled in America after the war.

3 Yitskhok Rudashevski, age 15, kept his diary in a ghetto in Lithuania. He wrote about studying and learning with other young people in the ghetto. He and his family did not survive.

4 Miriam Korber was born in Romania. She wrote her diary at age 18 in a ghetto in Ukraine. She became a doctor after the war.

5 **6** Petr Ginz and Eva Ginzova were brother and sister. They both wrote diaries in a ghetto called Terezin. Petr made many works of art there, too. He was killed in a concentration camp at age 15. Eva survived and became an artist.

A Changed World

Anne Frank was one of millions of people killed during the Nazi genocide (JEN-uh-side). We call this event in history the Holocaust (HOL-uh-kost).

Tower of Faces at the United States Holocaust Memorial Museum

After the war, world leaders decided to learn from the past. They punished as many of the killers as they could. They worked to understand how the Holocaust happened. And they made laws to try to stop it from happening again.

Our world is not perfect. But we do not stop trying. We study the past to learn from our mistakes. We remember those who were killed in the Holocaust. And we work to make the world better and safer for all of us.

Words to Know

GENOCIDE: The planned killing of a group of people because of who they are or what they believe

HOLOCAUST: The Nazi-organized killing of Jews and other people in Europe during World War II

Glossary

CONCENTRATION CAMP:
A place where Nazis held Jews and others. Many people were killed or died there.

GENOCIDE: The planned killing of a group of people because of who they are or what they believe

GHETTO: A closed-off area, usually in a Polish town or city, where the Nazis forced Jews to live together

JEWS: Those born into a Jewish family or who practice the religion of Judaism

LIBERATE: To set free

DEFEAT: To win a war, battle, or contest against a person, group, or country

DICTATOR: A leader who makes all the rules for a country and controls its people

HOLOCAUST: The Nazi-organized killing of Jews and other people in Europe during World War II

INVADE: To enter and try to take over a place, often by force

NAZIS: A group of people who followed the ideas of a German leader named Adolf Hitler

SEGREGATE: To separate someone or something from others

47

Index

Bold page numbers
indicate illustrations.

A
Auschwitz–Birkenau
camp 32, **32–33,**
33, 39, 40

B
Bergen-Belsen camp
34, 40, 41

C
Concentration camps
32–33, 32–34, **35,**
36, 43, 46, **46**

F
Feigl, Peter 43, **43**
Frank, Anne
  capture and arrest
    32
  in concentration
    camps 32, 33, 34,
    40, 41
  death 34, 41
  diary 6–7, 15,
    28–31, **31, 38,**
    38–41
  life in hiding 21,
    22, 25–28, 30
  school days 14, 15
Frank, Edith 8, **8,** 33,
  34, 40

Frank, Margot 8, **8,**
  14, 20–22, 25, 33,
  34, 40, 41
Frank, Otto 8, 34, **34,**
  39, 40, 41

G
Genocide 44, 45, 46
Ghettos 42, 43, 46, **46**
Gies, Miep 24, **24,** 39
Ginz, Petr 43, **43**
Ginzova, Eva 43, **43**
Great Depression 13

H
Hitler, Adolf 4–6, **9,**
  9–10, 16, 36, 47, **47**
Holocaust 44, 45, 47

J
Judaism 5, 46

K
Kleiman, Johannes **24**
Korber, Miriam 43,
  43
Kugler, Victor **24**

N
Nazis
  anti-Semitism 10
  leader 4, 5, 9, 10,
    47
  soldiers **6, 10–11**

symbol 10, **10**

P
Pfeffer, Fritz 25, **25,**
  34

R
Rudashevski, Yitskhok
  43, **43**

S
Secret Annex 21,
  22–23, 22–25, **27,**
  38, 39, **41**

T
Time line 38–41

V
van Pels family 22, 27,
  34
Voskuijl, Bep 24, **24**

W
Wolf, Otto 42
World War II 16–19,
  36–37, 45, 47